ANTS

CRABTREE
PUBLISHING COMPANY
WWW.CRABTREEBOOKS.COM

CRABTREE
PUBLISHING COMPANY
WWW.CRABTREEBOOKS.COM

Published in Canada
Crabtree Publishing
616 Welland Avenue
St. Catharines, ON
L2M 5V6

Published in the United States
Crabtree Publishing
PMB 59051
350 Fifth Ave, 59th Floor
New York, NY 10118

Published in 2020 by Crabtree Publishing Company

First published in Great Britain in 2019 by Wayland
Copyright © Hodder and Stoughton, 2019

Printed in the U.S.A./122019/CG20191101

Author: Susie Williams

Editorial director: Kathy Middleton

Editors: Victoria Brooker, Ellen Rodger

Designer: Lisa Peacock

Illustrator: Hannah Tolson

Production coordinator and prepress: Margaret Salter

Print coordinator: Katherine Berti

Library and Archives Canada Cataloguing in Publication

Title: Ants / by Susie Williams and [illustrated by] Hannah Tolson.
Names: Williams, Susie, author. | Tolson, Hannah, illustrator.
Description: Series statement: What lives in the dirt? |
  Previously published: London: Wayland, 2019. | Includes index.
Identifiers: Canadiana (print) 20190195061 |
  Canadiana (ebook) 2019019507X |
  ISBN 9780778773863 (hardcover) |
  ISBN 9780778773955 (softcover) |
  ISBN 9781427125019 (HTML)
Subjects: LCSH: Ants—Juvenile literature.
Classification: LCC QL568.F7 W55 2020 | DDC j595.79/6—dc23

Library of Congress Cataloging-in-Publication Data

Names: Williams, Susie, author. | Tolson, Hannah, illustrator.
Title: Ants / by Susie Williams and Hannah Tolson.
Description: New York : Crabtree Publishing Company, 2020. |
  Series: What lives in the dirt? | Includes index.
Identifiers: LCCN 2019043625 (print) | LCCN 2019043626 (ebook)
  ISBN 9780778773863 (hardcover) |
  ISBN 9780778773955 (paperback) |
  ISBN 9781427125019 (ebook)
Subjects: LCSH: Ants--Juvenile literature.
Classification: LCC QL568.F7 W629 2020 (print) |
  LCC QL568.F7 (ebook) | DDC 595.79/6--dc23
LC record available at https://lccn.loc.gov/2019043625
LC ebook record available at https://lccn.loc.gov/2019043626

What Lives in the Dirt?

ANTS

By Susie Williams and Hannah Tolson

Ants live together in groups.

A group can be made up of 100 ants
or sometimes thousands of ants!

Each group is called a colony.

Ants are **insects**. Like all insects,
their body is made up of three parts:
a head, a thorax, and an abdomen.

abdomen

claw

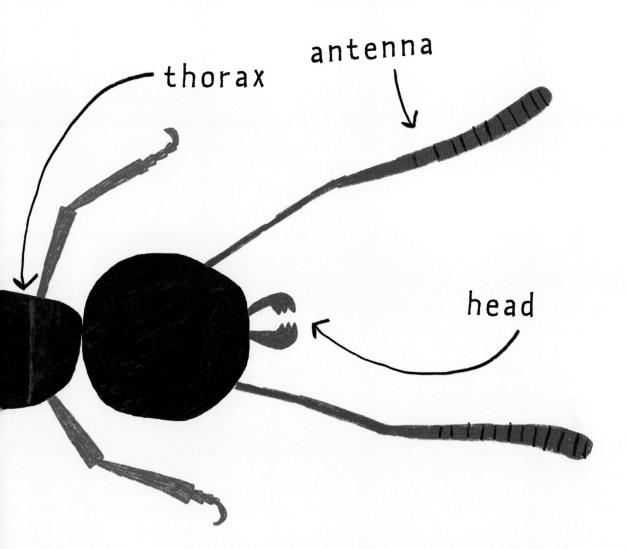

thorax

antenna

head

Long antennas on their head help them feel
their way around. At the end of each leg is
a hooked claw that is used for climbing.

Ants build their home, called a
nest, in soil, in trees, or in walls.

In the nest, ants dig a lot
of tunnels that connect
different rooms.

8

Some rooms are used to store food
and some are used as resting places.

Each colony contains three types of ants:
the queen, the female workers,
and the males.

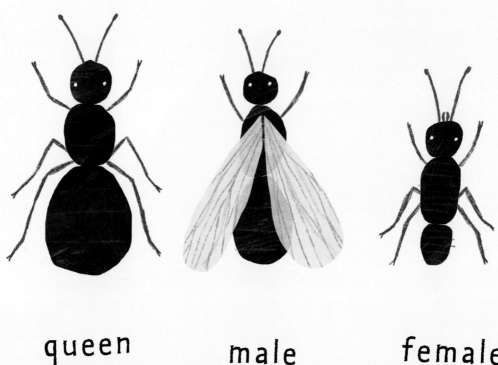

queen

male

female
worker

Usually, all the ants you can see
are female worker ants.

They do the jobs that are needed to keep
the colony healthy, such as finding food
or removing waste.

11

When ants go out of the nest, they leave behind a trail of **scent** so they can find their way back home.

Look for ants traveling
in a straight line from
their nest to some food.

Ants don't have ears. Instead, ants feel **vibrations** through their feet.

These vibrations help them to know if danger is coming.

Beetles, birds, and spiders
like to eat ants.

Humans have one stomach,
but ants have two!

One stomach holds their food.

The second stomach holds
food that they keep to
share with other ants.

Ants have parts called
mandibles that are like jaws.

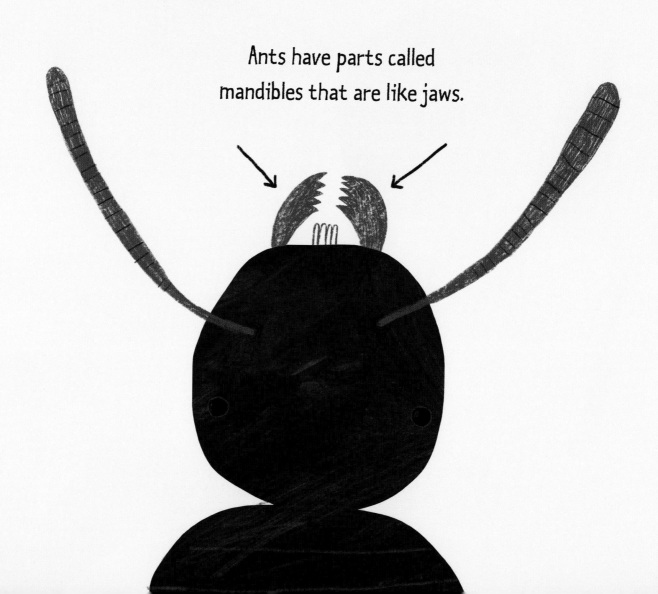

Mandibles are used for holding and carrying,
biting, cutting, digging, fighting, and hunting.

Ants will eat almost anything they can find,
from fruit and vegetables to
dead animals or **fungus**.

There are many different types of ants.
Most ants are usually black,
brown, yellow, or red.

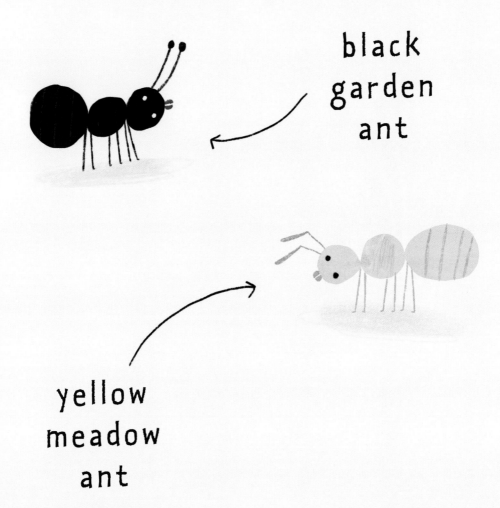

black
garden
ant

yellow
meadow
ant

But some ants around the world can
be green or **metallic**.

metalic
green ant

velvet
ant

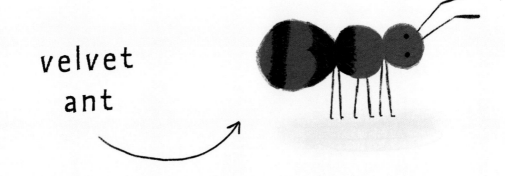

Black garden ants are harmless
and won't bite or sting.
But red ants will sting you
if they feel threatened.

Some ants have terrifying names such as
fire ant and bullet ant, because of the pain
caused when they sting you.

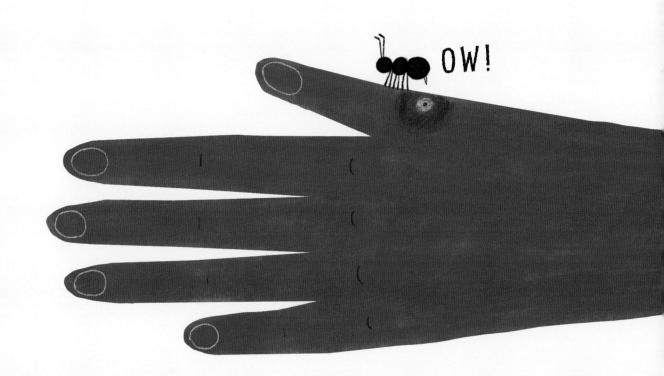

OW!

Ants play an important role in nature.
The tunnels they make in the soil help
water and **oxygen** reach the roots
of plants and help them grow.

Ants also take seeds down tunnels.
Some of these seeds sprout and grow
into new plants. See if you can spot any
busy ants and watch them as they work.

Build an ant farm

Watch ants up close and see how they build their nests.

1. Put the small jar, with its lid on, inside the large jar.

2. Get soil from where you find your ants. Fill the space between your two jars with soil. Loosen the dirt so it is not stuck together. The soil should not be too dry (your ants will dry out) or too wet (your ants will drown). Leave 1/2–1 inch (2–3 cm) of empty space at the top of the jar.

3. Find some ants! Check that the ants are garden ants and not ants that will bite or sting you. Brown or black ants should be fine.

4. Using a spoon, gently scoop some ants inside the jar. Aim to get 20–25 ants from the same colony. Cover the jar with a lid and ask an adult to punch small holes in the lid to allow air in so the ants can breathe.

You will need:

- one large glass jar with lid
- one small glass jar with lid that fits inside the large jar
- cotton balls
- honey or jam or fruit
- soil

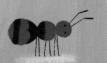

If the holes are too large, the ants will crawl out. Don't use cloth to cover the jar. The ants will chew through it and escape.

Always handle the jar gently and never, ever shake it.

5. Put the jar in a warm place, but away from direct sunlight. Feed the ants with a few drops of jam, honey, or small pieces of fruit.

6. Don't pour water into the jar. If the soil looks too dry, add a wet cotton ball inside the top of the jar.

7. Ants prefer to tunnel at night, so put a dark cloth over the ants when you aren't watching.

You should soon start to see some amazing tunnels!

After a week, return the ants to their nest.

More amazing facts about ants

Scientists have estimated that there are between 1 and 10 quadrillion (10,000,000,000,000,000) ants alive today.

There are more than 12,000 different **species** of ants.

Ants don't have lungs. Instead, they take in oxygen through small holes in the sides of their bodies.

Ants are super strong. One ant can lift more than 20 times its own body weight. That's like you being able to lift up a car!

Glossary

antennas – A pair of long, thin body parts on the head of insects and other animals that are used to help them sense or feel

fungus – Something that grows on dead material, such as mushrooms growing on dead logs

insect – A small animal with a hard covering over its body

metallic – Looks like metal

oxygen – A gas that plants and animals need to breathe

scent – A smell

species – A class or group of animals that share common characteristics

vibrations – Small, quick movements

Index